NARROW GAUGE BRANCH LINES

ROMNEYRAIL

Vic Mitchell
and
Keith Smith

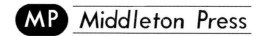

MP Middleton Press

First Published May 1999
Reprinted September 2002

ISBN 1 901706 32 X

© Middleton Press, 1999

Design   Deborah Esher
Typesetting   Barbara Mitchell

Published by
          Middleton Press
          Easebourne Lane
          Midhurst, West Sussex
          GU29 9AZ
Tel: 01730 813169
Fax: 01730 812601

Printed & bound by Biddles Ltd,
          Guildford and Kings Lynn

CONTENTS

ACKNOWLEDGEMENTS

We are immensely grateful to Messrs G.A.Barlow and J.B.Snell for sharing their great knowledge of the line with us. We would also like to express our gratitude to R.M.Casserley, G.Croughton, A.French, N.Langridge, Mr D.and Dr S.Salter, J.J.Smith and to the photographic contributors. The help from our wives is recorded with deep sincerity.

Location map showing adjacent railways as in 1938-47. (Railway Magazine)

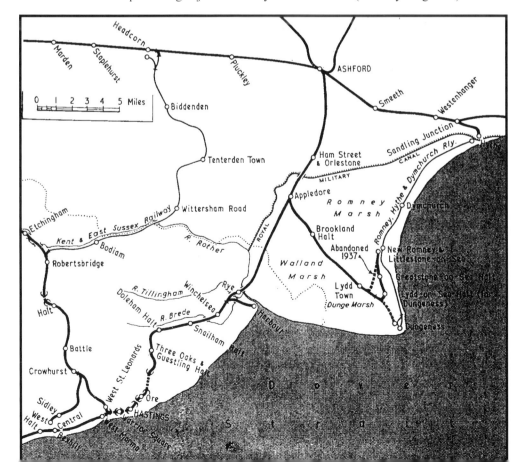

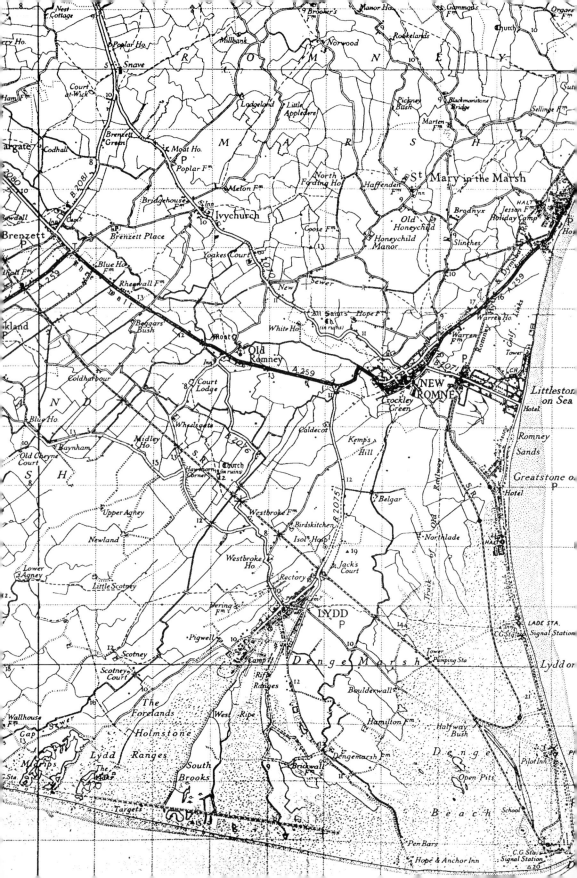

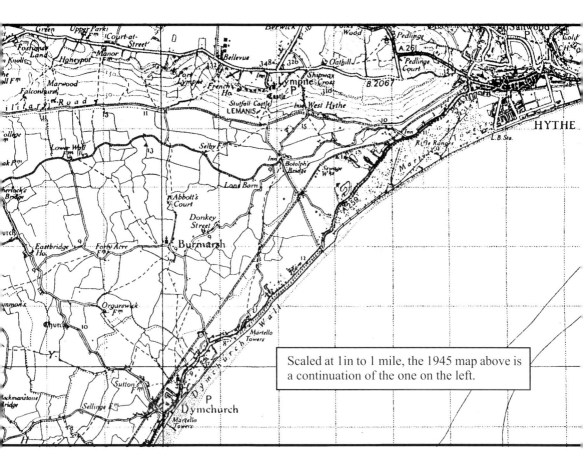

Scaled at 1in to 1 mile, the 1945 map above is a continuation of the one on the left.

GEOGRAPHICAL SETTING

South-east England is bounded by a horizontal horseshoe of Chalk, the ends of which form the White Cliffs of Dover and Beachy Head. Inside this are parallel ridges of Sandstone which, in the north, form cliffs at Hythe and Sandgate. Within these structures is yet a third horseshoe, this being Wealden Clay. It is relatively flat and comes to the coast, in the north, as Romney Marsh, between Hythe and New Romney.

South of New Romney is a unique peninsular formed of shingle and known as Dungeness. Almost totally infertile, its size increases annually as marine rounded flints are transported from the eroded cliffs of the South Downs in the Beachy Head area.

Romney Marsh has been traditionally a Summer grazing area for sheep and Dungeness has been a source of shingle. The coast of the area presented fine recreational beaches and it was this feature that was the main reason for the construction of the line.

The station maps are at the scale of 25ins to 1 mile, but those for New Romney and Hythe are not available in their entirety.

HISTORICAL BACKGROUND

The South Eastern Railway's main line from London to Folkestone was completed in 1843 and it was from this that branches were opened between Ashford and Hastings in 1851 and between Sandling, Hythe and Sandgate in 1874. From the former branch, a line was built south from Appledore to Dungeness, this opening to goods (mainly shingle) in 1881 and to passengers in 1883. It was extended northwards to New Romney in the following year. The lines were operated by the South Eastern & Chatham Railway from 1899, the Southern Railway from 1923 and British Railways (Southern Region) from 1948.

In the early 1920s, two wealthy gentlemen were looking for a suitable area in which to create a new miniature railway, which could also serve as a useful public railway. The SR suggested that the Dymchurch area was remote from their stations and that there was good potential for the development of holiday traffic, in view of the splendid deserted sandy beaches.

Work started in 1926 on the construction of a 15ins. gauge railway, under a Light Railway Order (belatedly!). The central character in this unique scheme was Captain J.E.P.Howey whose family had created an immense fortune in Australia during the development of Melbourne. Traffic commenced between Hythe and New Romney on 16th July 1927. The name "Romney, Hythe & Dymchurch Railway" was chosen, making it one of the few lines to announce its stations in the incorrect order.

Extension onto the barren and almost uninhabited wastes of Dungeness was well advanced before the public enquiry for a LRO was held in March 1928, the entire route being laid as double track. It was opened as far as The Pilot on 24th May 1928 and to Dungeness during the first weekend of August of the same year.

The holiday trade was buoyant until the outbreak of World War II in September 1939, but a

normal service was maintained until May 1940, albeit mainly for military personnel and locals deprived of petrol. The latter were mostly evacuated from the district and the railway was requisitioned for military use in June 1940. It conveyed vast numbers of troops between the various camps on the route and the Hythe-New Romney section saw regular trains throughout most of the duration of the War, but the southern section was used thus only until about 1942. In the latter part of the War it conveyed steel pipes to Lade in connection with PLUTO (Pipe Line Under The Ocean), a submarine petrol supply for the Allied armies.

The line was derequisitioned in July 1945 and the northern section was reopened on 1st March 1946, albeit Saturdays only at first. The New Romney to Maddieson's Camp length came back into use on 1st August following, but the route to Dungeness remained closed until 21st March 1947. Only a single track was available south of New Romney from that date.

Holiday traffic returned, but the 1960s brought serious problems: overseas resorts became increasingly attractive, Howey died in 1963 and two retired bankers acquired control in 1964, much of the equipment and infra-structure was life expired and a move to a new site was considered in 1969. The RH&DR Supporters Association was formed in 1967 to help solve the problems.

Truncation of the route was an option assessed and total closure was proposed in 1971. Salvation came in February 1972, when control passed to a group of railway-minded businessmen not seeking a return on their capital, but preferring to assist in creating a long-term future for the enterprise. A contract for the year-round conveyance of school children between the Dymchurch area and New Romney was secured in 1977, this helping to tip the balance in favour of survival. It has helped this unique miniature steam and diesel operated main line to run successfully throughout the 1980s and 1990s, with its one-third full size stock.

The bold outline of the Hythe Beds is the background as a construction train sets out across Romney Marsh. Few railways used express locomotives for such purposes. (RHDR coll.)

PASSENGER SERVICES

The first full Summer timetable showed a train almost hourly, daily. A Winter service of five or six trains daily was maintained north of New Romney until 1940, with one or two extended to Greatstone and two Saturday trains to Dungeness in some years. The severe Winter of 1946-47 was the last to have trains advertised, and then it was Saturdays only.

The peak holiday periods in the 1930s were often provided with up to 12 trains on the northern section, with three extended to Dungeness and many extra workings as necessary.

Named trains were introduced in the 1930s; famous after World War II were "The Bluecoaster Limited", "The Coronation Limited" and finally "The Marshlander". Initially they ran non-stop, but they were limited-stop in some years. Although the southern section was single, the service frequency increased in the 1950s.

By 1973, the peak timetable had 15 trains, six of which ran to Dungeness. The Summer of 1986 saw nine return trips between Hythe and Dungeness, plus a few short workings.

Service frequency has always been carefully tailored to meet anticipated traffic demands.

July 1928

THE PILOT, LITTLESTONE-ON-SEA, DYMCHURCH, and HYTHE.—Romney, Hythe, and Dymchurch.

July 1929

DUNGENESS, NEW ROMNEY, DYMCHURCH, and HYTHE.—Romney, Hythe, and Dymchurch.

NOTES.

All trains will stop to set down at Botolphs Bridge, and Lade, on notice being given to Guard at previous Station, and will take up from there on request.

November 1930

DUNGENESS, NEW ROMNEY, DYMCHURCH, and HYTHE.—Romney, Hythe, and Dymchurch.

Miles		Week Days and Sundays.					
		mrn	mrn	aft	aft	aft	aft
	Dungeness (Light House) ..dep.	..	..	..	..	..	**S**
1	The Pilot	....	....	....	....	....	..
4	Greatstone	..	..	1 40	..	5 20	....
5	**New Romney**	9 30	11 5	2 0	3 30	5 30	7 30
7	Holiday Camp	9 38	1113	2 8	3 38	5 38	7 38
8¾	**Dymchurch**	9 45	1120	2 15	3 45	5 45	7 45
9¾	Burmarsh Road	9 50	1125	2 20	3 50	5 50	7 50
13¼	**Hythe** (Kent) 322, 330 ....arr.	10 0	1135	2 30	4 0	6 0	8 0

Miles		Week Days and Sundays.					
		mrn	non	aft	aft	aft	**S**
	Hythe (Kent) ....dep.	1030	12 0	2 45	4 30	6 30	9 0
4	Burmarsh Road	1040	1210	2 55	4 40	6 40	9 10
5	**Dymchurch**	1045	1215	3 0	4 55	6 45	9 15
6¾	Holiday Camp	1052	1222	3 7	4 52	6 52	9 22
8¾	**New Romney 347**	11 0	1230	3 15	5 0	7 0	9 30
9¾	Greatstone	....	1236	....	5 20	....	....
12¾	The Pilot ....[347	..	..	..	..	..	..
13¾	**Dungeness** (Light House) arr.	....	....	....	....	....	....

S Sats. only.

☞ All trains will stop to set down at Lade, Botolphs Bridge, on notice being given to Guard at previous Station, and will take up from there on request.

August 1934

DUNGENESS, NEW ROMNEY, DYMCHURCH, and HYTHE—Romney, Hythe, and Dymchurch

Miles	**Down**	Week Days and Sundays.											
		mrn	mrn	mrn	mrn	aft	non	aft	aft	aft	aft	aft	aft
	Dungeness (Lgt. House) dp	..	..	**R**	..		12 0		..		4 30	6 0	**R**
1	The Pilot	....	....	....	....	....	12 5	....	....	....	4 35	....	....
—	Maddieson's Camp	..	..	..	..	..	1210	..	..	..	4 40	..	..
4	Greatstone	....	....	....	....	....	1215	....	....	....	4 45	....	....
5	**New Romney**	9 30	1015	1035	1110	1210	1225	1 10	2 10	3 10	4 55	6 18	8 0
7	**Holiday Camp**	9 38	1023	1043	1118	1218	1232	1 18	2 18	3 18	5 2	6 25	8 8
8¾	**Dymchurch**	9 45	1030	1050	1125	1225	1245	1 25	2 25	3 25	5 15	6 35	8 15
9¾	**Burmarsh Road**	9 50	1035	1055	1130	1230	1250	1 30	2 30	3 30	5 20	6 40	8 20
13¼	**Hythe** (Kent) 330....arr.	10 0	1045	11 5	1140	1240	1 0	1 40	2 40	3 40	5 30	6 50	8 30

Miles	**Up**	Week Days and Sundays.											
		mrn	mrn	non	aft	aft	aft	aft	aft	aft	**R**	aft	**R**
	Hythe (Kent) ....dep.	1030	11 0	12 0	1 0	2 0	2 45	4 30	6 0	6 30	7 0	7 30	9 0
4	Burmarsh Road	1040	1110	1210	1 10	2 10	2 55	4 40	6 10	6 40	7 10	7 40	9 10
5	**Dymchurch**	1045	1115	1215	1 15	2 15	3 0	4 45	6 15	6 45	7 15	7 45	9 15
6¾	Holiday Camp	1052	1122	1222	1 22	2 22	3 7	4 52	6 22	6 52	7 22	7 52	9 22
8¾	**New Romney 347**	11 0	1130	1230	1 30	2 30	3 15	5 0	6 30	7 0	7 30	8 0	9 30
9¾	Greatstone	11 6	....	....	....	....	3 21	....	....	....	....	....	....
—	Maddieson's Camp	1111	..	..	..	..	3 26	..	..	..	..	..	..
12¾	The Pilot. ....[347	1118	....	....	....	....	3 33	....	....	....	....	....	....
13¾	**Dungeness** (Lgt. House) dp	1130	..	..	..	..	3 45	5 20	..	..	..	..	..

Extra Trains (if required) on Week-days and Sundays.—Dymchurch to Hythe at 12 noon, 2, 3 5, 3 45, 4 30, 5 20, and 5 45 (stopping at Burmarsh Road); and Hythe to Dymchurch at 11 30 mrn., 1 30, 2 30, 3 15, 4, 4 50, and 5 15 aft. (stopping at Burmarsh Road). **R** Runs if required

December 1938

DUNGENESS, NEW ROMNEY, DYMCHURCH, and HYTHE—Romney, Hythe, and Dymchurch.

Miles	**Down**	Week Days only.							
	(Lgt. House)	mrn	mrn	mrn	aft	aft	aft	aft	
		Saturdays only.	Except Saturdays.	Sats. only.	Saturdays only.	Except Saturdays.		Saturdays only.	
	Dungeness ....dep.	9 0	..		1 30	..	..	7 30	..
1	Pilot	9 5	....		1 35	....	....	7 35	....
—	Lade	9 10	9 55		1 40	1 45	..	7 40	..
2¼	Maddieson's Camp	9 15	10 0		1 45	1 50	....	7 45	....
4	Greatstone .... [stone	9 20	10 5		1 50	1 55	..	7 50	..
5	NewRomney & Little-	9 30	1015	1130	2 0	2 0	5 30	8 0	....
7	Holiday Camp (Jesson)	9 38	[illegible]	1138	2 8	2 8	5 38	8 8	..
8¼	**Dymchurch**	9 45	1031	1145	2 15	2 15	5 45	8 15	....
9¼	Burmarsh Road	9 50	1035	1150	2 20	2 20	5 50	8 20	..
14	**Hythe** (Kent) 330. arr.	10 0	1045	12 0	2 30	2 30	6 0	8 30	....

Up	Week Days only.							
	mrn		aft	aft	aft	aft	aft	aft
	Sats. only.		Saturdays only.	Except Saturdays.		Except Saturdays.	Saturdays only.	Sats. only.
Hythe (Kent) ......dep.	1030	....	1230	1230	4 30	6 30	6 30	9 0
Burmarsh Road	1040	..	1240	1240	4 40	6 40	6 40	9 10
Dymchurch	1045	....	1245	1245	4 45	6 45	6 45	9 15
Holiday Camp (Jesson)	1052	..	1252	1250	4 50	6 50	6 50	9 22
New Romney & Little-	11 0	....	1 0	1 0	5 0	7 0	7 0	9 30
Greatstone ..[stone 347		..	1 5	1 10	....	7N5	7 5	
Maddieson's Camp		....	1 10	1 15	....	7N10	7 10	
Lade		..	1 15	1 30	..	7N15	7 15	
Pilot..[(Lgt. House)347		....	1 20	....	....	....	7 20	
Dungeness ....arr.		..	1 30	..	..	..	7 30	

N Runs when required.

1 August to 15 September 1946

	a.m.	a.m.	p.m.	p.m.	p.m.	p.m.	p.m.	p.m.	p.m.	p.m.	p.m.	S.O.	S.O.
Hythe ... ... dep.	**10 30**	**11 30**	**12 30**	**2 00**	**2 30**	**3 00**	**3 45**	**4 30**	**5 30**	**6 00**	**6 40**	**8 30**	**10 30**
Burmarsh Rd. dep.	10 45	11 45	12 45	2 15	2 45	3 15	4 00	4 45	5 45	6 15	6 55	8 45	10 45
Dymchurch dep.	**10 55**	**11 55**	**12 55**	**2 25**	**2 55**	**3 25**	**4 10**	**4 55**	**5 55**	**6 25**	**7 05**	**8 55**	**10 55**
St. Mary's Bay dep.	11 00	12 00	1 00	2 30	3 00	3 30	4 15	5 00	6 00	6 30	7 10	9 00	11 00
New Romney dep.	**11 10**	**12 10**	**1 10**	**2 40**	**3 10**	**3 40**	**4 25**	**5 20**	**6 10**	**6 40**	**7 20**	**9 10**	**11 10**
Greatstone ... dep.	...	...	1 20	...	...	...	...	5 30	...	7 05	...	9 20	11 20
Maddieson's Camp ... arr.	...	...	1 25	...	...	...	...	5 35	...	7 10	...	9 25	11 25
Lade ... ... dep.	...	...	...	...	...	...	...	...	...	...	...	...	...
Pilot ... ... dep.	...	...	...	...	...	...	...	...	...	...	...	...	...
Dungeness ... arr.	...	...	...	...	...	...	...	...	...	...	...	...	...

	a.m.	a.m.	a.m.	p.m.	p.m.	p.m.	S.S.	p.m.	p.m.	p.m.	p.m.	p.m.	S.O.	S.O.
Dungeness ... dep.	...	...	...	...	...	...	...	...	...	...	...	...	...	...
Pilot ... ... dep.	...	...	...	...	...	...	...	...	...	...	...	...	...	...
Lade ... ... dep.	...	...	...	...	...	...	...	...	...	...	...	...	...	...
Maddieson's Camp ... dep.	...	10 10	...	...	...	1 40	2 15	...	...	...	...	5 35	7 10	9 25
Greatstone ... dep.	...	10 15	...	...	...	1 45	2 20	...	...	...	...	5 40	7 15	9 30
New Romney dep.	**9 30**	**10 30**	**11 30**	**12 40**	**1 30**	**2 00**	**2 30**	**3 00**	**3 30**	**4 00**	**4 45**	**5 50**	**7 30**	**9 50**
St. Mary's Bay dep.	9 40	10 40	11 40	12 50	1 40	2 10	2 40	3 10	3 40	4 10	4 55	6 00	7 40	...
Dymchurch dep.	**9 50**	**10 50**	**11 50**	**1 00**	**1 50**	**2 20**	**2 50**	**3 20**	**3 50**	**4 20**	**5 05**	**6 10**	**7 50**	...
Burmarsh Rd. dep.	9 55	10 55	11 55	1 05	1 55	2 25	2 55	3 25	3 55	4 25	5 10	6 15	7 55	...
Hythe ... ... arr.	**10 10**	**11 10**	**12 10**	**1 20**	**2 10**	**2 40**	**3 10**	**3 40**	**4 10**	**4 40**	**5 25**	**6 30**	**8 10**	...

S.O.—Saturday only. **S.S.**—Saturdays and Sundays only.

	a.m.	a.m.	p.m.	p.m.	p.m.	p.m.	p.m.	p.m. S.O.	p.m. S.O.
Hythe	10 30	11 30	12 40	2 00	3 00	4 30	6 00	7 30	8 30
Burmarsh Road*	10 45	11 45	1 00	2 15	3 15	4 45	6 15	7 45	8 45
Dymchurch	10 55	11 55	1 05	2 25	3 25	4 55	6 25	7 55	8 55
St. Mary's Bay*	11 00	12 00	1 10	2 30	3 30	5 00	6 30	8 00	9 00
New Romney ...	11 10	12 10	1 20	2 40	3 40	5 10	6 40	8 10	9 10
New Romney	—	—	1 30	—	5 20	6r50	8r15	9r15	
Greatstone	—	—	1 35	—	5 25	6r55	8r20	9r20	
Maddieson's Camp ...	—	—	1 40	—	5 30	7r00	8r25	9r25	
Lade	—	—	—	—	—	—	—	—	
Pilot	—	—	—	—	—	—	—	—	
Dungeness	—	—	—	—	—	—	—	—	

	a.m. A S.O.	a.m.	a.m.	p.m.	p.m.	p.m.	p.m.	p.m. S.O.	p.m.
Dungeness	—	—	—	—	—	—	—	
Pilot	—	—	—	—	—	—	—	
Lade	—	—	—	—	—	5 45	—	
Maddieson's Camp ...	8 50	10 15	—	1 45	—	5 50	—	
Greatstone	8 55	10 20	—	1 50	—	—	—	
New Romney ...	9 00	10 30	11 30	12 30	2 00	3 00	4 30	6 00	7 30
St. Mary's Bay* ...	9 10	10 40	11 40	12 40	2 10	3 10	4 40	6 10	7 40
Dymchurch	9 15	10 50	11 50	12 50	2 20	3 20	4 50	6 20	7 50
Burmarsh Road ...	9 20	10 55	11 55	12 55	2 25	3 25	4 55	6 25	7 55
Hythe	9 35	11 10	12 10	1 10	2 40	3 40	5 10	6 40	8 10

A—" The ABC Minors Special."
r—Runs if required.
S.O.—Saturdays only.
*—Stops only on notice being given to the driver.

		SO a.m.	SX a.m.	a.m.	a.m.	p.m.	p.m.	p.m.	p.m.	p.m.	p.m.	p.m.
Dungeness ...	dep.	—	—	9§55	—	12 00	—	1§55	—	4 15	—	5 45
Pilot	dep.	—	—	10§00	—	12 05	—	2§00	—	—	—	5 50
Lade	dep.	—	—	10§10	—	12 15	—	2§10	—	—	—	6 00
Maddieson's Camp ...	dep.	—	—	10 15	—	12 20	1‡45	2§15	—	—	—	6 05
Greatstone ...	dep.	—	—	10 20	—	12 25	1‡50	2§20	—	—	—	6 10
New Romney {	arr.	—	—	10 25	—	12 30	1‡55	2§25	—	4 35	—	6 15
	dep.	9 00	9 30	10 30	11 50	12 35	2 00	2 30	3 30	4 40	5 35	6 20
St. Mary's Bay {	dep	9 10	9 40	10 40	12 00	12 45	2 10	2 40	3 40	4 50	5 45	6 30
Dymchurch ... {	arr.	9 15	9 45	10 45	12 05	12 50	2 15	2 45	3 45	4 55	5 50	6 35
	dep.	9 18	9 48	10 48	12 08	12 53	2 18	2 48	3 48	4 58	5 58	6 38
Burmarsh Road ...		9*22	9*52	10*52	12*12	12*57	2*22	2*52	3*52	5*02	6*02	6*42
Hythe	arr.	9 35	10 05	11 05	12 25	1 10	2 35	3 05	4 05	5 15	6 10	6 55

		a.m.	a.m.	p.m.	p.m.	p.m.	p.m.	p.m.	p.m.	p.m.	SO p.m.
Hythe	dep.	10 30	11 30	12 40	2 00	2 45	3 30	4 30	5 30	6 30	8 30
Burmarsh Road ...		10*44	11*44	12*54	2*14	2*59	3*44	4*44	5*44	6*44	8*44
Dymchurch ... {	arr.	10 48	11 48	12 58	2 18	3 03	3 48	4 48	5 48	6 48	8 48
	dep.	10 50	11 50	1 00	2 20	3 05	3 50	4 50	5 50	6 50	8 50
St. Mary's Bay ...		10 55	11 55	1 05	2 25	3 10	3 55	4 55	5 55	6 55	8 55
New Romney {	arr.	11 05	12 05	1 15	2 35	3 20	4 05	5 05	6 05	7 05	9 05
	dep.	11 10	—	1 20	—	3 25	—	5 10	—	—	9†10
Greatstone ...	dep.	11 15	—	1 25	—	—	—	5 20	—	—	9†15
Maddieson's Camp ...	dep.	11 20	—	1 30	—	—	—	5 25	—	—	9†20
Lade	dep.	11 25	—	1§35	—	—	—	5 30	—	—	9†25
Pilot	dep.	11 35	—	1§45	—	—	—	5 35	—	—	9†35
Dungeness ...	arr.	11 40	—	1§50	—	3 45	—	5 40	—	—	9†40

§ or SO—Saturdays and Bank Holidays Only. † —Runs Only for Passengers from New Romney and
‡ or SX—Not Saturdays. *—Stops by Request Only. Beyond.

		a.m.	a.m.	a.m.	a.m.	a.m.	p.m. SX	p.m. SO	p.m.	p.m. A	p.m.	p.m.	p.m.
Dungeness ...	dep.	—	—	9§55	—	12 00	—	1 55	—	3 45	—	5 00	—	7 00
Pilot	dep.	—	—	10§00	—	12 05	—	2 00	—		—		—	7 05
Lade	dep.	—	—	10§10	—	12 15	—	2 10	—		—		—	7 15
Maddieson's Camp ...	dep.	—	—	10 15	—	12 20	1‡45	2 15	—		—		—	7 20
Greatstone ...	dep.	—	—	10 20	—	12 25	1‡50	2 20	—	"Bluecoaster Limited"	—		—	7 25
New Romney {	arr.	—	—	10 25	—	12 30	1‡55	2 25	—		—	5 26	—	7 30
	dep.	9 00	9 30	10 30	11 50	12 35	2 00	2 30	2 30	3 00	4 30	5 30	6 00	7 35
St. Mary's Bay ...		9 10	9 40	10 40	12 00	12 45	2 10	2 40	2 40	3 10	4 40	5 40	6 10	7 45
Dymchurch {	arr.	9 15	9 45	10 45	12 05	12 50	2 15	2 45	2 45	3 15	4 45	5 45	6 15	7 50
	dep.	9 18	9 48	10 48	12 08	12 53	2 18	2 48	2 48	3 18	4 48	5 48	6 18	7 53
Burmarsh Road ...		9*22	9*52	10*52	12*12	12*57	2*22	2*52	2*52	3*22		4*52	5*52	6*22	7*57
Hythe	arr.	9 35	10 05	11 05	12 25	1 10	2 35	3 05	3 05	3 35	4 30	5 05	6 05	6 35	8 10

		a.m.	a.m.	p.m.	p.m.	A p.m.	p.m.	p.m.	p.m.	p.m.	p.m.	p.m.	SX p.m.	SO p.m.
Hythe	dep.	10 30	11 30	12 40	2 00	2 30	3 00	3 30	4 30	5 30	6 30	7 30	8 30	8 30
Burmarsh Road ...		10*44	11*44	12*54	2*14		3*14	3*44	4*44	5*44	6*44	7*44	8*44	8*44
Dymchurch {	arr.	10 48	11 48	12 58	2 18		3 18	3 48	4 48	5 48	6 48	7 48	8 48	8 48
	dep.	10 50	11 50	1 00	2 20	"Bluecoaster Limited"	3 20	3 50	4 50	5 50	6 50	7 50	8 50	8 50
St. Mary's Bay ...		10 55	11 55	1 05	2 25		3 25	3 55	4 55	5 55	6 55	7 55	8 55	8 55
New Romney {	arr.	11 05	12 05	1 15	2 35		3 35	4 05	5 05	6 05	7 05	8 05	9 05	9 05
	dep.	11 10	—	1 20	—		4 10	—	6 10	—	—	—	9†10	
Greatstone ...	dep.	11 15	—	1 25	—		—	—	6 15	—	—	—	9†15	
Maddieson's Camp ...	dep.	11 20	—	1 30	—		—	—	6 20	—	—	—	9†20	
Lade	dep.	11 25	—	1§35	—		—	—	6 25	—	—	—	9†25	
Pilot	dep.	11 35	—	1§45	—		—	—	6 35	—	—	—	9†35	
Dungeness ...	arr.	11 40	—	1§50	—	3 15	—	4 30	—	6 40	—	—	—	9†40

§ or SO—Saturdays and Bank Holidays Only. † —Runs Only for passengers from New Romney
SX—Not Saturdays. and Beyond.
*—Stops by Request Only. A—Supp. Fare Train, all seats Bookable in Advance.
The " Bluecoaster Limited."

Miles		a.m	a.m	a.m	a.m	non		p.m	p.m	p.m	p.m	p.m	p.m		p.m	p.m	p.m	p.m	p.m	p.m	p.m	p.m	
		A	B					A	B	A	B	B	A		A	B	A	A	B	A	B	A	
	Dungeness..........dep	..	..	..	..	12 0	..	..	1 45	2 0	3 0	3 15		3F55	4 15	4 35	4 45	..	5 45	5 50	7 0	..
3	Maddieson's Camp.....	9 15	..	1015	..	1215	..	1 30	1 45	2 0	2 15	..		..	..	..	5 0	..	6 0	6 5	7 15	..
4	Greatstone.............	9 20	..	1030	..	1220	..	1 35	1 50	2 5	2 20	..		..	..	..	5 5	..	6 5	6 10	7 20	..
5	New Romney .... arr	9 25	..	1025	..	1225	..	1 40	1 55	2 10	2 25	3 20	3 35		4 35	4 55	5 10	..	6 10	6 15	7 25	..
	dep	9 30	9 30	1030	1130	1230	..	1 45	2 0	2 15	2 30	3 30	3 40		4 40	5 0	5 15	5 30	6 15	6 20	7 30	..
7	St. Mary's Bay	9 38	9 38	1038	1138	1238	..	1 53	2 8	2 23	2 38	3 38	3 48		4 48	5 8	5 23	5 38	6 23	6 28	7 38	..
8	Dymchurch...... arr	9 43	9 43	1043	1143	1243	..	1 55	2 12	2 28	2 43	3 43	3 53		4 53	5 13	5 28	5 43	6 28	6 33	7 42	..
	dep	9 45	9 45	1045	1145	1245	..	2 0	2 15	2 30	2 45	3 45	3 55		4 55	5 15	5 30	5 45	6 30	6 35	7 45	..
13	Hythe............. arr	1010	1010	11 5	12 5	1 10	..	2 20	2 35	2 45	3 5	4 5	4 10		4F40	5 15	5 35	5 50	6 5	6 50	7 0	8 10	..

		a.m	a.m		p.m	p.m		p.m	p.m	p.m	p.m	p.m	p.m	p.m	p.m	p.m	p.m	p.m	p.m	p.m			
								A	B	A	A	B	A	B		A	N	P				
	Hythe.............dep	1030	1130	..	1230	2 0	..	2F30	2 45	2 50	3 30	3 30	4 30	5 30	5 30	6 20	7 30	8 30	8 30			
5	Dymchurch....... arr	1050	1145	..	1245	2 15	..	3	0 3	5 3	45 3	45	4 45	5 45	5 50	6 45	7 45	8 50	8 50	..	..
	dep	1053	1148	..	1248	2 18	..	3	3 3	7 3	48 3	48	4 48	5 48	5 53	6 48	7 48	8 53	8 53	..	..
6	St Mary's Bay	1058	1153	..	1253	2 23	..	3	8 3	12 3	53 3	53	4 53	5 53	5 58	6 53	7 53	8 58	8 58	..	..
8	New Romney .... arr	1110	12 5	..	1 5	2 35	..	3	20 3	25 4	5 4	5	5 6	6 10	7 5	8 5	9 10	9 5	..	..
	dep	1115	1225	..	1 10	2 38	..	3	25 3	35 4	10	..	5 8	6 10	6X15	7X10	8X10	9X15	9X10	..	..
9	Greatstone........	1120	1230	..	1 15		..	..		..		..	5 13	6 15	6X20	7X15	8X15	9X20	9X15	..	..
10	Maddieson's Camp.....	1125	1235	..	1 20		..	..		..		..	5 18	6 20	6X25	7X20	8X20	9X25	9X20	..	..
13	Dungeness.......... arr	1140	..	:	1 35	2 53	..	3F15	3 45	3 55	4 30	..	5 35	6 35							

A Runs 27th June to 18th September only	F Supplementary fares payable. All seats bookable in advance. Observation car attached	P Saturdays only. Will not run 27th June to 18th September
B Will not run 27th June to 15th September	N Runs daily from 27th June until 21st August, then Saturdays only until 18th September	X Only conveys passengers from New Romney and beyond.

LOCOMOTIVES

Although the track gauge was approximately one-quarter of standard gauge, most of the locomotives were about one-third the size of their main line cousins. They were loosely modelled on the London & North Eastern Railway's class A1 4-6-2 express passenger engines and five were built between 1925 and 1927 by Davey, Paxman and Co. Ltd. Two 4-6-2s of Canadian outline were completed in 1931 by the Yorkshire Engine Company and numbered 9 and 10. Two 4-8-2s, which were of freelance design but closely resembled the LNER Pacifics and were intended for ballast traffic, came from Paxman's works in 1927. They were nos 5 and 6.

No.	Original name	Notes	Picture no.
1	*Green Goddess*		22, 116
2	*Northern Chief*		26, 33, 46, 49, 55, 77, 88
3	*Southern Maid*		4, 10, 39, 41, 82, 84, 85, 96, 104
4	*The Bug*		43
5	*Hercules*		11, 20, 28, 40, 71, 81, 87, 95, 105
6	*Samson*		19, 31, 35, 45, 87
7	*Typhoon*		18, 54, 81, 83
8	*Hurricane*	a	36, 79
9	*Doctor Syn*	b	9, 67, 75, 115, 118
10	*Black Prince*	c	32, 33, 71, 75, 79, 109, 115, 118
11	*Black Prince*	d	16, 78, 93

a. *Bluebottle* 1938 to 1946
b. *Winston Churchill* from 1948
c. *Doctor Syn* from 1949
d. From 1976

Locos 9 and 10 exchanged names more than once before the War owing to Howey's wish to always have a *Doctor Syn* in traffic. *Southern Maid* was originally *Southern Chief* but was delivered nameless as were *Hercules* and *Samson* which were named, at first, *Man of Kent* and *Maid of Kent*.

The first internal combustion locomotive had a Ford Model T engine and arrived in 1928. It was intended for use on Winter trains but was too slow. Captain Howey's 1914 Rolls Royce Silver Ghost was shorn of its shooting brake body in 1930 and adapted for rail use, the work being completed in November 1932.

1a. At the rear of the Rolls Royce there were four 25ins diameter wheels, all driven, while there was a bogie at the front. The lengthened chassis was braced with trusses, necessary at the 60mph that it is reputed to have achieved. (Lens of Sutton)

1b. The match boarding of the cab was extended around the petrol tank and vacuum pipes were strung along the frame untidily. Other changes include larger headlights and a bonnet from another vehicle. The locomotive worked most of the Winter trains from 1933 to 1940. A chain linked the rear axles outside the wheels. (RHDR coll.)

1c. A cab to complement the saloon coaches was built in 1946 and a Ford lorry engine was fitted in 1947, the new radiator being fitted under the cowl. It had carried the cowcatcher from its inception and was broken up in 1961. The photograph, which dates from 1947, does not show that it had a sliding roof, of value when shunting in reverse. (J.C.Flemons)

HYTHE

2. As was the custom at many large railway termini, arrival and departure platforms were considered appropriate. Gentlemen stand on the former, while ladies wait on the latter, one appearing to be a shopper. The lines on the left lead to the turntable, beyond which an engine shed was built later. (Lens of Sutton)

3. The scissors crossing visible in front of the signal box was removed in 1928. On the left is the single storey refreshment building and on the right is the staff bungalow. This was sold in 1947. (Lens of Sutton)

4. No. 3 *Southern Maid* stands at platform 2 on 1st June 1929. It is coupled to four of the original four-wheeled coaches which were very unsatisfactory and thus short lived. The train shed was almost doubled in length in 1933. (LGRP/NRM)

Blue Coaster Express. Romney, Hythe & Dymchurch Railway.

5.   The restaurant received a second storey in about 1930 and subsequently dwarfed the station. Some of the first coaches can be seen standing at platform 4 and a milk churn awaits transport. (Lens of Sutton)

6.   The stock of "The Bluecoaster Limited" is being propelled into platform 3. This named train ran from 1947 to 1951 and reached Dungeness non-stop in 45 minutes. Fishermen enjoy the otherwise useless Royal Military Canal, which is described in *Kent & East Sussex Waterways* (Middleton Press). The footbridge from which this picture was taken was demolished in 1963. (Lens of Sutton)

7.   The pre-war ballast hoppers and ramp were repaired and fitted with an electric winch in 1946, a year before this photograph was taken. The Romney Marsh Ballast Co. Ltd unloaded Dungeness shingle here until 1948, trains running early in the morning or during the evening. (H.C.Casserley)

8.   A 1958 view includes the crossovers (which were of a larger radius than those seen in picture no. 3), the original 30ft turntable (which had been replaced by a 40ft one in 1951), a ballast wagon (which was once one of a fleet of 60) and the footbridge mentioned earlier. (F.Hornby)

9.   On one of the busiest days of 1969, August Bank Holiday, no. 9 *Winston Churchill* split the points on its approach to the terminus. The absence of facing point locks meant that a fragment of wood went undetected. The service continued with only two platforms. (RHDR coll.)

10.   No. 3 *Southern Maid*, with a tender larger than its original, rests after arrival at platform 2 on 15th June 1978. The centre line is for engine release - the connection to it from the track at platform 3 was added in 1927-28. Coach no. 806 was one of eight 16-seaters completed in 1962-69. (T.Heavyside)

right

12.   A 1997 photograph shows only one lever out of use and thus painted white. There is full interlocking but no distant signal; instead there is an outer home. (P.G.Barnes)

11.   Running into platform 3 on 1st April 1986 is no. 5 *Hercules*. Colour light signals had been installed in 1966, but two semaphores were put back in 1975. The track at platform 4 was removed at that time, as was the adjacent engine release loop. (T.Heavyside)

far right

13.   The locomotive shed seen in picture no. 8 was adapted for the manufacture of miniature locomotives by Crowhurst Engineering. One of their products is seen in July 1997. (P.G.Barnes)

14.   A new frontage for the station was built in 1971-72 and is seen in 1997. The former "Light Railway Restaurant" had also been extended substantially, but was no longer railway property, having been sold in the early years. (P.G.Barnes)

SOUTH OF HYTHE

15.   Leaving Hythe on 11th April 1982 is the Ravenglass & Eskdale Railway's 4-6-4 diesel hydraulic *Shelagh of Eskdale.* Built in 1969, this locomotive came south for a year's service on the school train while the RHDR was having a diesel built. RHDR steam engines were on the RER in 1925, 1971 and many times since. (D.Trevor Rowe)

16.   About one mile from Hythe, the line passes under the road to West Hythe. A halt was provided here in 1927-28, it being known as "Prince of Wales Halt", after a nearby inn. Working the 4.20pm from Hythe on 25th August 1980 is 4-6-2 no. 11 *Black Prince.* (S.C.Nash)

17.   Another RER diesel to run briefly on the RHDR was the Bo-Bo *Lady Wakefield* of 1980. She is seen approaching Botolph's Bridge from Hythe on 5th October 1980. (D.Trevor Rowe)

18.   Approaching Botolph's Bridge is no. 7 *Typhoon* hauling the 6.20 Hythe to New Romney service on 17th June 1978. There was a halt at the nearby level crossing until about 1938; it had a wooden shelter. (T.Heavyside)

19.   The hot Summer of 1947, combined with some massive rail creep, caused severe track deformation between Botolph's Bridge and Burmarsh Road. No. 6 *Samson* was able to proceed cautiously to New Romney, despite its rigid eight-coupled wheels. (RHDR coll.)

20.   Burmarsh Road Halt was in use until 11th October 1947, having been demoted from a station at a very early date. A wooden shelter was provided on the down side. No. 5 *Hercules* was fitted with a light for working trains in the evening and is seen southbound. The platforms have been used again since 1977, but only by children as this is the terminal point for school trains. A bus link to Burmarsh is provided. (D.Collyer coll.)

DYMCHURCH

21.   Looking south soon after the opening, we see the bay platform (left) at which many trains from New Romney were expected to terminate. The bay loop ran to a turntable which was situated behind the signal box, visible beyond the roof. (Lens of Sutton)

22.   No. 1 *Green Goddess* waits to proceed to Hythe with a rake of uncomfortable four-wheelers in about 1927. Note that the bridge abutments double as toilets. (Pamlin Prints)

23.   Lower right is the line used by engines leaving the turntable and returning to their trains in the bay platform. The bay loop was removed in 1929, as the traffic developed in a way that avoided the need to terminate trains here from New Romney. The turntable was taken out soon after. The Hythe - Dymchurch shuttles operated for some years after 1946, but engines had to run tender-first in one direction. (Lens of Sutton)

24.   This view from the footbridge includes a train at the bay platform and another conveying milk churns. The building on the right became staff accommodation, having been completed in 1928. It was used as a refreshment room until about 1933. (E.A.Beet)

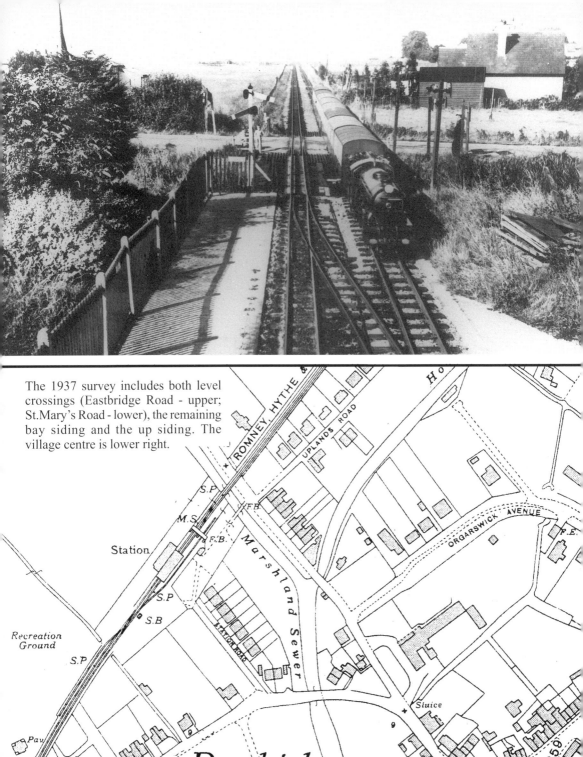

The 1937 survey includes both level crossings (Eastbridge Road - upper; St. Mary's Road - lower), the remaining bay siding and the up siding. The village centre is lower right.

25. Looking towards Hythe from the footbridge we can observe economy in signal posts and the north crossover. Less obvious is Marshland Sewer, which passes under the leading coach. (Lens of Sutton)

26. *Northern Chief* was involved in a collision on Eastbridge Road when travelling from Hythe sometime in the 1930s. *Southern Maid* dived into the dyke at exactly the same point in 1946, but on that occasion the lorry driver was killed. (A.L.S.Richardson)

27. A 1937 panorama includes the points for both sidings, the southern crossover, the staff bungalow and the signal box, which contained 16 levers. There was no weed killing train at that time. (NRM)

28.	The Somerset Light Infantry was posted to the area in 1940 and quickly sent *Hercules* and two of the six ex-RER bogie ballast wagons to the SR's Ashford Works for fitting with armour plate. Two Lewis guns and a Boyes anti-tank rifle were installed on their return. (D.Collyer coll.)

29.	The inclined floors left a wedge shaped void at each end, there were no brakes and the buffers were not standard. The train was kept in a siding near Burmarsh Road under camouflage, with the locomotive in steam, until Autumn 1941. Both photographs were taken on 23rd September 1940. (D.Collyer coll.)

30. A post-war motor scooter stands with parents of Sunday School children, as they prepare for their outing to one of the fine beaches served by the line. Also of interest is the down side building, seldom recorded in full, and the lack of steps to the east span of the footbridge, by then redundant. (D.Collyer coll.)

31. It is post-war boom time as *Samson* blows off on its way to Hythe. The 4-8-2s were little used in the 1930s, but worked hard subsequently. Wartime troop trains often required two locomotives. A fleet of 56 new saloon coaches replaced the four-wheelers in 1935-36. (V.Mitchell coll.)

32.   Now we have two views from 25th April 1947. First we see the crossover set for no. 10, then *Black Prince*, to gain the up road after having passed permanent way work. Also evident is a 10¼ins gauge line which was soon to be moved to Hastings. (H.C.Casserley)

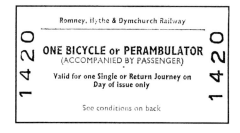

33.   No. 10 is departing for Hythe as no. 2 *Northern Chief* arrives. Earlier views show both signals on one post. It is thought that the Army erected the post on the right. The Canadian locomotives had higher cabs with sliding roofs, ideal for Winter work. (H.C.Casserley)

34. The RHDR Association was involved in the reconstruction of the station in 1977. First, the down side was cleared. The doors and windows seen in picture 24 had been covered with thick concrete (right) by the Army. This wall was retained. (RHDR coll.)

———————▶

35. No. 6 *Samson* passes over the rather stagnant sewer on 14th June 1978, as it works the 2.20pm from Hythe. As road traffic increased, so did accidents at the level crossings. All 13 were fitted with automatic flashing lights between 1974 and 1985. (T.Heavyside)

———————▶

36. The up siding and both colour light signals are featured in this record of no. 8 *Hurricane* approaching the station with the 4.55pm from Dungeness on 18th April 1992. The rear of the train will be close to St. Mary's Road crossing. (S.C.Nash)

Another Train is Coming
if Lights Continue to Flash

37.   After the trials with RER diesels, Romneyrail decided to adopt the same power source. This is the first such engine to be ordered, it being built by TMA Engineering in 1983. No. 12 *John Southland* is seen near the end of the up siding on 18th April 1992. (S.C.Nash)

38.   The unnamed no. 14 is hauling the 3.35pm Hythe to Dungeness on 1st August 1995. Another TMA product, it arrived on the line in 1989 and also has Bo-Bo wheel arrangement. (J.Scrace)

39.   Part of the new down side building can be spotted as no. 3 *Southern Maid* pauses with the 10.35 New Romney to Hythe service on 19th July 1997. The footbridge rests on the Gents, the second span having long gone. (P.G.Barnes)

40.   A short canopy was erected on the thick blast wall on the up side. No. 5 *Hercules* is speeding through with empty stock, hence the station master's raised thumb. The train would form the 70th Anniversary Special from Hythe on 19th July 1997. (P.G.Barnes)

41.   The 11.30 from Hythe on the same day rumbles over the watercourse, headed by no. 3 *Southern Maid*. The sign design is similar to that employed by the District Railway in the early part of the century. The crossover at this location had been removed in 1962. (P.G.Barnes)

42.   A 1998 photograph reveals that the original building was incorporated into the new design, it serving as a ticket office and shop. Fortunately the creators of the railway acquired sufficient land for a car park here. (P.G.Barnes)

JEFFERSTONE LANE

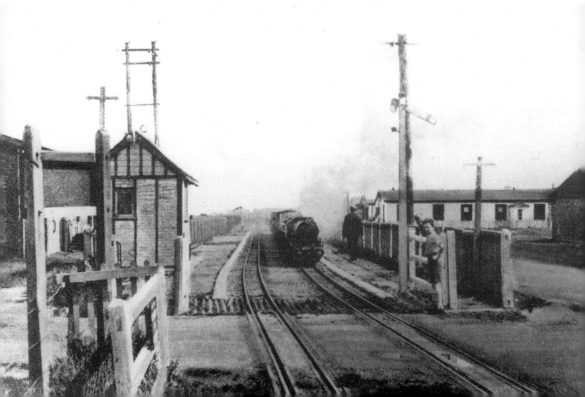

←

43.   No. 4 *The Bug* was built by Krauss in Munich to a standard design and delivered in May 1926 for use on construction trains. It is standing on a single line; the decision to use double throughout was made after work had started. It was sold in November 1933 to Kamiya of Blackpool and it eventually went to Belfast. (A.J.S.Richardson)

←

44.   Initially known as "Jesson Camp", the name was changed to "St. Mary's Bay" in 1946, although timetables simply showed "Holiday Camp" until that time. The platforms were built north of the lane to St. Mary's in the Marsh. The two signals were worked from a signal box behind the camera, but only for a short period. (Lens of Sutton)

45.   Some nearer-to-scale passengers admire no. 6 *Samson* at the head of a long train from Hythe. In the background is the spacious shelter, not recorded in other views. (Unknown)

46.   The line now forms the western boundary of the residential area of St. Mary's Bay for over one mile. Despite this, the station was renamed "Jefferstone Lane" on 9th April 1981. *Northern Chief* is seen on 5th September 1977. (J.Scrace)

47.   A 1998 snap from a southbound train reveals that the up side buildings had been replaced by a simple modern structure. There is substantial school traffic at this location. (P.G.Barnes)

SOUTH OF JEFFERSTONE LANE

48.   One of the many bridges found by the new owners to be seriously defective was known as the "Duke of York's". It was a substantial lattice structure but had to be cut up and replaced by girders. They are seen being decked on 9th April 1968. The name "Collins' Bridge" was applied subsequently, after one of the co-owners at that time. (G.A.Barlow)

49.   No. 2 *Northern Chief* had left Hythe at 4.20pm on 5th September 1976 and is seen crossing Collins' Bridge. By that date, many of the coach frames were being extended to receive their third body. (J.Scrace)

ROMNEY, HYTHE & DYMCHURCH RAILWAY
ST. MARY'S BAY to
NEW ROMNEY
(PASSENGER TICKET ONLY)
SINGLE FARE
See Conditions on back
23747

Romney Hythe & Dymchurch Rly
DYMCHURCH (Marshlands) to
Holiday Camp
(Jesson)
(Passenger Ticket Only)
SINGLE   FARE
See Conditions on back
0519

50.   The Warren Bridge carries the A259 over the line and advertises the railway well to touring motorists. It had to be strengthened for the construction traffic for Dungeness "C" Power Station. The new girders no longer rest on the central pier. (A.R.W.Crowhurst)

51.   Romneyrail was able to assist contractors by conveying new sewer pipes in 1978-79. The Simplex arrived from the Eaton Hall Railway in 1947 and was changed from petrol to diesel in 1967. It is seen from Warren Bridge with Littlestone water tower and the coastal houses in the background. (P.Hawkins)

52.   Visiting locomotives have been major features of May Galas in recent years. Coming from "Down Under" on a short visit, this model of a 2ft gauge Tasmanian K1 class 0-4-0+0-4-0 Beyer Garratt ran with the coach once used by the Queen. The whistle had to be removed during the passage under Warren Bridge in 1993. (G.A.Barlow)

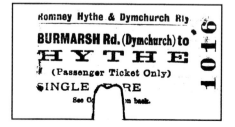

53.   Looking north from the same bridge on 14th May 1995, we can enjoy the appearance of the Bure Valley Railway's no. 7 *Spitfire*, a 2-6-2 built by Winson Engineering in 1994. Its design is based on the 2ft 6ins gauge Indian class ZB locomotives. (D.Trevor Rowe)

54.   Drifting snow provided operating difficulties on 2nd March 1986, when one road was submerged. No. 7 *Typhoon* is approaching The Warren. (P.H.Groom)

NEW ROMNEY

55.   Construction of the railway was still proceeding in 1926, but the Duke of York (who was crowned King George VI in 1937) requested a visit. This is the scene on 5th August 1926, as the crowds are kept behind the fences as *Northern Chief* and a short train are prepared to fetch the Duke and his party from St. Mary's Bay. An amazing 105 of these four-wheelers were built. (RHDR coll.)

←————

56.   The station was designed as a terminus, the arrival platform and engine release road being on the left. On the right is a carriage siding and the departure line. Confusingly, the station showed the name "Littlestone-on-Sea" for a short period, it being on the boundary of Littlestone and New Romney. (Lens of Sutton)

←

57.   The exterior presented a unique styling to the prospective passenger. The reason for the place names being in the wrong order in the railway's name was that it simply sounded better that way! (RHDR coll.)

←

58.   Clayton Wagons Ltd built eight superb bogie coaches in 1928, these being unofficially termed "Pullmans". The end compartments were for luggage and the lighting batteries. The steam heating ceased to be of value when the Rolls Royce was introduced on Winter services. Their height was reduced in 1934, when the tunnnel floors were raised due to flooding. (Clayton Wagons)

59.   Reverse curves were deliberately put in the main line (left) for improved visual effect! The turntable was replaced by a 30ft one in 1936-37, which had previously served the Lynton & Barnstaple Railway. The shed on the right was occupied by Jackson, Rigby Ltd who were contracted to do the mechanical repair work for the first year or so. The scene was recorded on 1st June 1929. (LGRP/NRM)

60.　The workshop was well equipped, with power coming from an oil engine via the shafting and the belts visible. The firm was formerly located at Shalford and was experienced in the manufacture of miniature railway equipment. The RHDR bought the business in 1929. (RHDR coll.)

61.　Although the arriving locomotive is blurred due to its speed, this photograph is included as it shows the carriage shed (left), a bracket signal and the yard signal, all of which were short lived, being swept away by the realignment of 1929. (Lens of Sutton)

62.　Of even shorter life was the paint shop (left). It had three tracks, connected by a quadrant. Both this shed and the one beyond for carriages were dismantled to allow the unnecessary curves to be removed and straight track to be laid to the Dungeness extension in 1929-30. (RHDR coll.)

63.   A June 1929 photograph has the original
arrival platform behind the fence on the left and
the down Dungeness platform left of centre. The
corresponding up platform was originally beyond
the tunnels. The exchange sidings with the SR
are on the right, one RHDR line entering the
transfer shed from this end and an SR one from
the other. (LGRP/NRM)

64.   The RER carried large amounts of crushed
granite but, when this traffic was transferred to
standard gauge in 1929, the RHDR bought their
six bogie wagons for stone traffic. The well
engineered vehicles had bottom discharge doors.
The hoppers were eventually replaced by 20-seat
coach bodies on five of the frames. The sixth
was a war casualty. (E.A.Beet)

65.   The new straight track and signalling is featured in this view towards Hythe. On the left is the shelter on the new up platform provided in 1934-35 for trains from Dungeness. Few stations can have been so drastically altered in their initial years. Glazing was added to some of the original coaches. (Lens of Sutton)

66.   A 1936 panorama has (from left to right) the unmoved signal box, the carriage sheds, one of the original platform lines, the new roof over the through tracks, the up platform from 1934-35 and the revised position of the up siding. No longer did it rise to meet the standard gauge siding. (NRM)

67.   No. 9 (then *Doctor Syn*) approaches with a train of saloons from Hythe on 1st September 1938. On the right is an articulated set which, unlike those running on the LNER at that time, has a single axle at the end. The signal box was fitted with 24 levers. (R.S.Carpenter coll.)

68.   The vacuum brake piping was fitted to one side for accessibility, as the bodies were so close. The common bogie principle was abandoned in Britain by the end of the 1960s, but appeared in Kent again 30 years later with the advent of Eurostar trains. (E.A.Beet)

69.   The railway's war effort took a new turn after the Normandy landings in 1944. The advancing forces required vast quantities of petrol and so PLUTO was devised (Pipe Line Under The Ocean). Steel pipes were brought by the SR to the siding in the background, welded in the shed in the background, loaded onto frames as seen (the carriage bodies having been destroyed) and conveyed to Lade, where pumps had been fitted into bungalows to disguise them. Owing to the many derailments, it was found more expedient to haul the pipes by crawler tractor, but this destroyed much of the track. (D.Collyer coll.)

←————

70.   After repairing the track, the railway received extensive national publicity by inviting Laurel and Hardy to reopen the Dungeness section on 21st March 1947. Olly is supporting himself on one of the two then new observation cars, aptly carrying the name *Pluto*. The other was called *Martello*, after an earlier military scheme in the district. One car can be glimpsed in picture no. 6, behind the engine. They were rebuilt in 1956 and 1966 respectively as conventional saloons. (RHDR coll.)

71.   Seen departing for Hythe in immaculate condition on 25th April 1947 is no. 10, then still *Black Prince*. No. 5 *Hercules* is carrying out its intended task, freight working. Empty stone wagons are being returned to the crusher, this traffic continuing to New Romney until 1951. (H.C.Casserley)

72.   Viewed on the same day is the running shed and a rake of coaches built hurriedly after the War on frames that had been stripped by the Army. Full size signals were obtained from the SR; others can be seen in the background of the top cover picture. (H.C.Casserley)

73.   This post-war scene includes part of the old arrival platform and the awkward footbridge that was required to link the other three platforms. This was erected in about 1951. Sheds came and went: picture 66 shows one standing in this area. The footbridge was moved nearer the entrance with the 1973 rebuilding of the station. (Lens of Sutton)

74.   This poor photo is included as it shows the short-lived framework erected on the vehicles seen in picture 72 to improve safety. The next step was to cover the structures with hardboard. In the background are examples of temporary post-war houses known popularly as "Prefabs". (Lens of Sutton)

75.   The locomotive shed lacked adequate smoke ventilation and was thus very grimy. The "Canadians" were supplied with the correct Vanderbilt type tenders, but these were replaced with more conventional bodies in the early 1960s. (Lens of Sutton)

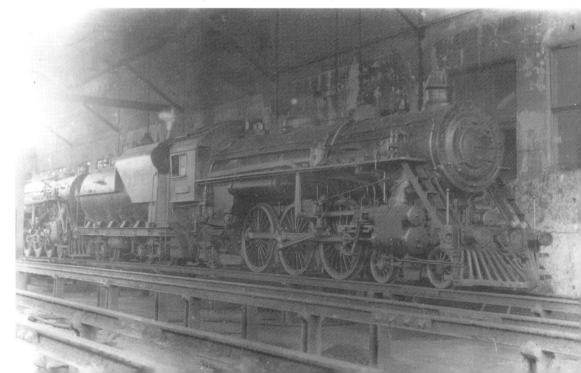

76.   Crossing the road, we see British Railways' terminus of the branch from Appledore and the point at which the RHDR became single after 1946. This was the site of the up platform until 1930 - a footbridge was provided over the double track (see inset), so that passengers could use the path on the left. The standard gauge crossed the road on the level to reach the RHDR yard. See our *Hastings to Ashford* album for details of the branch. (H.C.Casserley)

5144

R. H. & D. RLY
PLATFORM TICKET

DUNGENESS

Available for one hour.
Conditions of Issue
Holder of this ticket is subject
to Bye-laws, Regulations and
Conditions of the R. H. & D. Lt.
Rly. Co. The Company is not
under any conditions liable for
personal injury, loss, damage,
delay or detention to holder of
their luggage.
This ticket must be produced
and delivered up when
required and the Company
reserve the right to refuse
to admit holder to their
Platforms or require them to
leave the premises.

5144

77.   This 4-6-2 was built by Krupp in 1937 and is seen in the condition in which it arrived on the RHDR in 1976. It became no. 11 *Black Prince* and was extensively rebuilt in 1989. The building in the background houses carriages on the ground floor and a toy and model museum on the upper one. (RHDR coll.)

← ─────────

78.   The wall on the left was removed in the mid-1960s to allow the up platform to be extended toward the tunnels. The footbridge seen in picture 73 is in the background of this view of no. 2 *Northern Chief* about to leave for Dungeness on 4th June 1960. (F.Hornby)

79.   The track layout was changed for a third time when this spacious train shed was erected in 1973-74. A loop line is on the left, no. 8 has just arrived from Dungeness, no. 10 stands at platform 2 on the other through line waiting to start off to Hythe, and four carriage sidings are visible on the right. The date is 14th June 1978. (T.Heavyside)

← ─────────

80.   Until the advent of adequate diesel power in 1983, the school train required a steam locomotive at each end, as there is no run-round facility at Burmarsh Road. The Simplex was added on 15th February 1979, as this was the only engine to which the snow plough could be attached at that time. The carriage repair shop is in the left background. (RHDR coll.)

81.　　An April 1986 panorama shows the running lines to the left of the ash wagon, nos 5 and 7 being prepared, the new frontage to the engine shed and the paraffin tank is on the turntable. The turntable was returned to Devon to the Lynton & Barnstaple Railway Association in 1987 and a new one was built adjacent to the platforms. (T.Heavyside)

82.　　Drain cock steam spoils the appearance of no. 3 *Southern Maid* on 6th June 1992, but the photograph does give us the opportunity of looking the full length of the train shed, seeing the position of the footbridge since 1974 and also the reduced tunnel height when compared with picture 63. (M.Turvey)

83.　　The flat roofed extension in the background was added in about 1960, it allowing the entire locomotive fleet to be kept together. Note the "continuous pit" which makes the engines more accessible for minor repairs, such as changing brake blocks and springs. No. 7 *Typhoon* is seen on 12th May 1996. (P.G.Barnes)

84. A view from the footbridge on 19th July 1997 includes no. 3 *Southern Maid* taking water while working the 11.30 Hythe to Dungeness and also all four platforms. The down starting signal is largely obscured by a sighting board. All the 1962 colour light signals on the station itself had been replaced by electro-pneumatic semaphores in 1991-92. (P.G.Barnes)

85. The same locomotive is seen a few minutes later as it passes the site shown in the opposite direction in picture 76. The line on the right is a headshunt and on the left are industrial premises on the former BR station site. (P.G.Barnes)

86. Coach no. 1 has a body built on one of the original Hudson frames and was used by Her Majesty Queen Elizabeth II during her visit in 1957. Seen in 1997 is the 1987 turntable pit, the spacious carriage repair shop and (left) the old carpenter's shop. (P.G.Barnes)

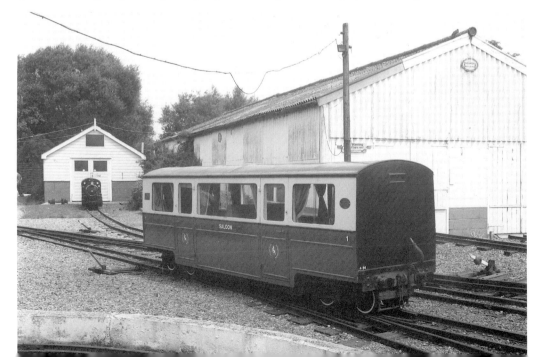

87. A rare combination of two 4-8-2s was recorded north of the station in May 1998, as *Hercules* and *Samson* ran non-stop Hythe-Dungeness-Dymchurch. The headboard is promoting Agfa film. (D.Trevor Rowe)

88. The erecting shop is situated on the opposite side of the running lines to the workshop. No. 2 *Northern Chief* is being tested on 19th July 1997, while *Redgauntlet* stands near the oil tank. (P.G.Barnes)

→

89. A glimpse into the erecting shop in 1998 includes the cab of one of the "Canadian" class. The hoist is able to lift a boiler, but the lack of road access means that it has to be taken by rail to the car park for loading onto a lorry. (P.G.Barnes)

90a.   Inside the machine shop in 1998 is a shaper (left), a lathe (concealed by its backplate), a milling machine and some newly turned wheels. In the roof are some relics of the original line shafting once used to drive all the machinery from one large power source. (P.G.Barnes)

top right
90b.   We now visit other areas not normally open to the public. A forge and grit blasting facilities are available in a separate building. (P.G.Barnes)

lower right
90c.   Access to the forge is via a turntable on the south side of the running shed. (P.G.Barnes)

VISITING LOCOMOTIVES

91.   Ex-German 0-8-0 60cm gauge no. 99.3461 was stored at New Romney in 1972-75. Intended for possible use on the Vale of Rheidol line, it was sold to the Froissy-Cappy-Dompierre Railway in France, where it is still running. This engine was built by Vulkan in 1925. (F.Hornby)

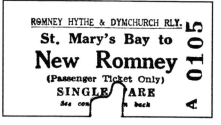

ROMNEY HYTHE & DYMCHURCH RLY.
St. Mary's Bay to
New Romney
(Passenger Ticket Only)
SINGLE FARE
See con . . . . n back

A 0105

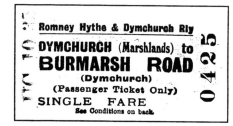

Romney Hythe & Dymchurch Rly
DYMCHURCH (Marshlands) to
BURMARSH ROAD
(Dymchurch)
(Passenger Ticket Only)
SINGLE FARE
See Conditions on back

0425

92.   18th September 1977. 4-4-2 *Count Louis* came from Fairbourne to take part in the RH&DR Golden Jubilee celebrations. This loco was built by Bassett-Lowke in 1924 and was their last 15ins gauge engine. (D.Trevor Rowe)

93.   15th October 1980. 4-6-2 *Rosenkavalier* arrived from Bressingham. The RHDR no. 11 *Black Prince* is behind. *Rosenkavalier* and *Mannertreu*, both at Bressingham, were originally identical with *Black Prince*, and all were built for an exhibition railway at Dusseldorf by Krupp in 1937. They are slightly larger than the more numerous and better known German 15ins gauge Pacifics by Krauss of Munich. (D.Trevor Rowe)

94.   5th October 1980. 2-8-2 *River Mite* from the Ravenglass & Eskdale Railway and built by Clarkson in 1966. (D.Trevor Rowe)

95.   2nd June 1985. 2-8-2 *River Esk* also from the RER and built by Davey Paxman in 1923. Coupled to it is RHDR no. 5 *Hercules*. (S.C.Nash)

96.　　19th May 1991. 0-8-2 *River Irt* from the RER and built in 1894 by Heywood as an 0-8-0T named *Muriel*. Also seen is RHDR no. 3 *Southern Maid*. (S.C.Nash)

97.　　13th September 1992. 4-6-0 *Sequoia* from USA and built in 1982 by Erich Thomsen for his Redwood Valley Railway, Berkeley, California. (D.Trevor Rowe)

98.   14th May 1995. 0-6-0 *Jack* from the Bredgar & Wormshill Railway near Maidstone and built for Jack Lemon-Burton in the 1960s. (P.G.Barnes)

99.   11th May 1997. 4-4-2 *Synolda* from the RER and built in 1912 by Bassett-Lowke. (D.Trevor Rowe)

100.   11th May 1997. 4-6-2 *Prince William* built by Trevor Guest for the Dudley Zoo Railway in the 1960s. (D.Trevor Rowe)

101.   11th May 1997. 0-4-0 American switcher from the BWR and built by Morse in 1950. (D.Trevor Rowe)

102.   10th May 1998. 0-4-2 *Bonnie Dundee* from Ravenglass which was originally a 2ft gauge Dundee gasworks 0-4-0T. Space precludes a comprehensive coverage of all visitors, but others can be seen in pictures 15, 17, 52 and 53. (P.G.Barnes)

GREATSTONE

103.   Known as "Greatstone Dunes" in its first years, the station had an eight-lever signal box, the roof of which is visible above the kiosk.   Although rodding was installed, the box may never have controlled the planned crossover and siding. Nothing remains at this site except the imprint of one canopy bracket in the cement of a wartime pillbox. The tank seen in this 1936 picture was moved to Hythe and the station was finally closed in 1977. (LGRP/NRM)

Daily

Miles		am SuX	am SO	am	am	pm	pm SO	pm	pm	pm	pm	pm	pm	pm	pm	pm
	Hythe .. .. .. dep	..	10 0	..	1030	11 45	..	1220	1 15	1 50	2 20	3 15	..	3 50 4 55	..	5 55 6 30	.. 7 0 7 45 .
5	Dymchurch		1018	..	1048	12 3	..	1238	1 33	2 8	2 38	3 33	..	4 8 5 13	..	6 13 6 48	... 7 18 8 3 .
6	St. Mary's Bay		1023	..	1053	12 8	..	1243	1 38	2 13	2 43	3 38	..	4 13 5 19	..	6 18 6 53	... 7 23 8 8 .
8	New Romney .... arr		1035	..	11 5	12 20	..	1255	1 50	2 25	2 55	3 50	..	4 25 5 30	..	6 30 7 5	... 7 35 8 20 ...
	New Romney .... dep	9 30	..	..	1110	12 25	..	1 0	..	2 30	3 0	3 55	..	.. 5 35	..	6J35	..
9	Greatstone.............	9 35	..	..	1115	12 30	..	1 5	..	2 35	3 5	4 0	..	.. 5 40	..	6J40	
10	Maddieson's Camp ..	9 40	..	..	1120	12 35	..	1 10	..	2 40	3 10	4 5	..	.. 5 45	..	6J45	
13	Dungeness .... arr	10 0	..	..	1140	12K55	..	1 30	..	3 0	3 30	4 25	..	.. 6 5			

Miles		am SuX	am SO	am	am	noon	pm FX	pm	pm	pm	pm	pm	pm	pm
	Dungeness .. .. dep	..	10 5	..	..	12 0	1 30	..	2 0	..	..	3 39	..	.. 4 25 .. 5 10 6 10 .. ..
3	Maddieson's Camp		1015	..	..	12 10	1 40	..	2 10	..	..	3 40	..	.. 4 35 .. 5 20 6 20 .... ..
4	Greatstone..		1020	..	..	12 15	1 45	..	2 15	..	..	3 45	..	.. 4 40 .. 5 25 6 25 .. ..
5	New Romney .... arr		1030	..	..	12 25	1 55	..	2 25	..	..	3 55	..	.. 4 50 .. 5 35 6 35 .. ..
	New Romney .... dep	9 30	..	..	1035 1130	12 30	..	..	2 0	2 30	3 15	4 0	.. 4 40 5 0 .. 5 45 6 45 .. ..
7	St. Mary's Bay	9 38	..	..	1043 1138	12 38	..	..	2 8	2 39	3 23	4 8	.. 4 48 5 8 .. 5 53 6 53 ..
8	Dymchurch	9 45	..	..	1050 1145	12 45	..	..	2 15	2 45	3 30	4 15	.. 4 55 5 15 .. 6 0 7 0 ..
13	Hythe .... arr	10 5	..	..	1110 12 5	1 5	..	..	2 35	3 5	3 50	4 35	.. 5 15 5 35 .. 6 20 7 20 .. ....

FX Fridays excepted.   **J** Only travels beyond New Romney if required.   **K** Does not travel beyond Maddieson's Camp on Fridays.   **SO** Saturdays only   **SuX** Sundays excepted

July 1956

ROMNEY SANDS

104.   Known initially as "Littlestone Camp", the station was "Maddieson's Camp" until 9th April 1981. Single track after World War II, a passing loop with island platform was brought into use in the Spring of 1974. No. 3 *Southern Maid* has just passed the combined ticket office and signal box on its way to Dungeness on 19th July 1997. (J.Petley)

105.   The rear coach is near the points of the loop as no. 5 *Hercules* heads for New Romney on 13th May 1995. The leading coach is the 32ft-long bar car no. 501, which carries 16 passengers plus an attendant and was built in 1977. (P.G.Barnes)

SOUND MIRROR BRANCH

As part of a scheme of experiments to improve the air defence of the country, an accoustical mirror was built at Hythe in 1923. This was intended to allow the sound of approaching airships or aircraft to be detected by means of a concrete structure having a concave face 20ft in diameter. Near its focal point was a horn that collected the air waves, these being piped to an operator wearing a stethoscope. The collector was movable, this enabling the orientation of the noise source to be calculated. This equipment was changed to microphones, amplifier and headphones in a later 200ft mirror.

The War Department proposed to construct three more similar devices further south at the time that the RHDR was being extended to Dungeness. An agreement was made for the conveyance of goods at 3s per ton, a passenger fare of 4d to the junction and special trains at £1.10s. There was also provision for the WD to use its own small locomotive bidirectionally on one line for personnel conveyance when RHDR trains were not operating. To this end, a shed was erected at Hythe and leased to the WD for housing its engine.

It was intended that the branch would be used for about 12 months, but it was actually in place for over 20 years. The freight returns for 1931 showed that the RHDR carried 891 tons that year, but in 1928 and 1931, for example, it was nearer 300. Almost all of this was associated with mirror construction, mainly sand and cement as there was plenty of stone on site. The railway carried only small amounts of coal and milk otherwise. However, the largest mirror was estimated to weigh 240 tons and so the figures are difficult to explain. The conveyance of formwork to and from the site would however, account for some tonnage.

A problem arose in 1937 when the SR decided to reroute its New Romney branch closer to the coast, in order to encourage building development. It encountered the temporary line that had become apparently permanent and was thus obliged to build a bridge over it. Needing silence, the mirror users were not happy with another railway in front of their equipment, not to mention the prospect of an urban area as well.

The mirrors were never used tactically and were officially abandoned in May 1939, although WD running powers to Hythe were retained. Radar took over and proved more effective, although the big mirror was apparently very successful at detecting trains leaving Calais Maritime station.

Driver Barlow claimed to be the last person to use the War Office siding, as it was officially known. His locomotive ran over a dog in about 1950 and the leading coach became derailed. The passengers helped rerail it with iron that the Army had abandoned in the area and the coach was pushed into the siding to await examination.

106. An aerial view from January 1930 has the RHDR parallel to the coast and the branch to the mirror site curving away from it. Access by road vehicle was impossible owing to the rounded shingle. The SR Appledore-Dungeness line is shown diagonally top left, with the New Romney branch curving to the right. (PRO)

107. The widths of the mirrors are from left to right: 200ft, 20ft and 30ft. Their distance from the coast was critical, to avoid collecting the sound of waves on the beach. They were completed in June 1930, July 1928 and April 1930 respectively. This is a 1994 view. (R.N.Scarth)

LADE

108.   The ground is almost entirely shingle south of Greatstone, as illustrated in this 1936 view. Only a few fishermen's huts and dwellings were to be found in the vicinity at that time. (LGRP)

109.   No. 10 *Doctor Syn* (a fictional smuggler) runs south on 13th August 1978 with its second tender. Some residential development had taken place by that time; more has happened since, but the halt was closed in 1977. (J.Scrace)

PILOT

110. The name was taken from the nearby Pilot Inn, which in turn was named after the men who navigated ships through the Straits of Dover. The desolate scene was recorded in 1936. The building was used as a dwelling by Driver Barlow in 1947 and demolished in 1968. Trains ceased to stop here after 1977. (LGRP)

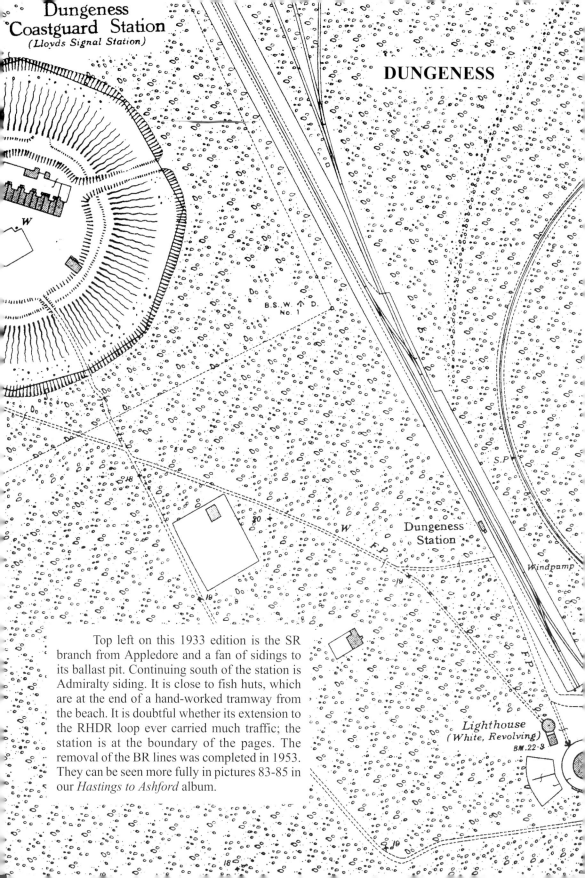

Dungeness Coastguard Station
(Lloyds Signal Station)

DUNGENESS

W

B.S.W. D.
No. 1

S.P.

W

Dungeness
Station

F.P.

Windpamp

*Lighthouse
(White, Revolving)*
BM.22·3

F.P.

Top left on this 1933 edition is the SR branch from Appledore and a fan of sidings to its ballast pit. Continuing south of the station is Admiralty siding. It is close to fish huts, which are at the end of a hand-worked tramway from the beach. It is doubtful whether its extension to the RHDR loop ever carried much traffic; the station is at the boundary of the pages. The removal of the BR lines was completed in 1953. They can be seen more fully in pictures 83-85 in our *Hastings to Ashford* album.

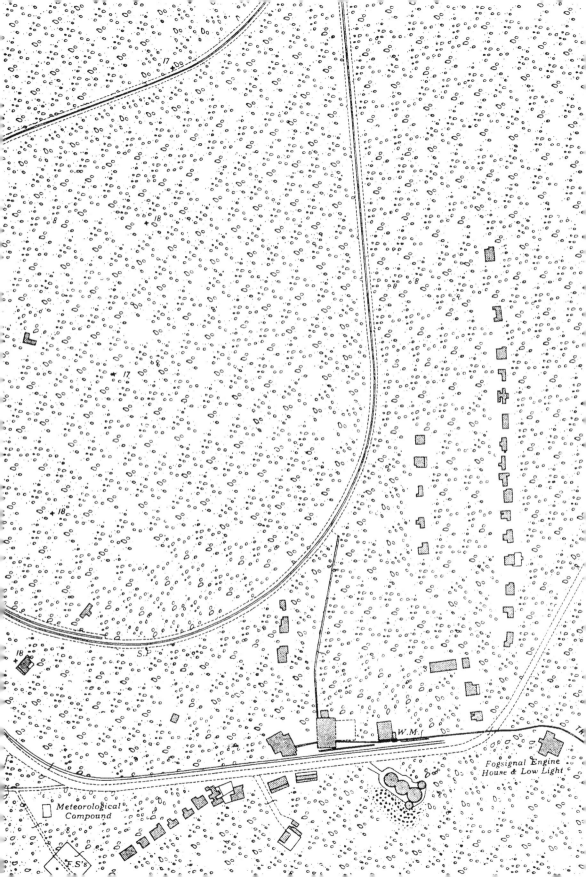

Meteorological
Compound

W.M.

Fogsignal Engine
House & Low Light

F.S's

111.   The RHDR's spacious refreshment room is seen in the 1930s, along with the SR platform (right). The latter had been visited by three trains each weekday until 4th July 1937. The small buildings are (from left to right) the ticket office, the toilets and the short-lived signal box. (LGRP/NRM)

112.   There was little to interest visitors at this windswept location other than birds and the lighthouse, which could usually be ascended. Partly devoid of blades, the wind pump had ceased to raise water for the locomotives by the time that this photograph was taken in the 1950s. (RHDR coll.)

113.   The uncluttered environs were ideal for stock photography in 1958. No. 205 was one of three wagons built in the late 1940s and adapted for passenger service. Behind it is no. 606, one of six semi-open 16-seaters built on Hudson frames in about 1950 and now part of history. (H.C.Casserley)

114.   No. 409 was a historic vehicle, having been constructed for the Duke of Westminster's Eaton Hall Railway in 1895. After reconstruction of that line was first mooted, in 1979, some of the vehicles from that source were returned there, including this one. (H.C.Casserley)

115.   On the left are the automatic Britannia points, where the terminal loop commences. Seen on 21st September 1969 is a then-rare train for enthusiasts. It was running non-stop from Hythe back to its starting point, behind nos. 10 and 9 which by then had matching tenders. (RHDR coll.)

116.   No. 1 *Green Goddess* was recorded in 1975, before the long wind shelter was blown over and destroyed. Extension and rebuilding of the coaches was a continuous activity, aluminium being used extensively in recent years. (D.Mitchell)

117.   Nos. 12 or 14 normally work the school train with a driving trailer coach at the opposite end. However, both were coupled to almost all the rolling stock on 16th May 1993. There were 54 coaches, the total weight being over 130 tons. In the background is the Dungeness Nuclear Power Station complex, which includes a visitor centre. (P.H.Groom)

118.   The siding was in use on 29th August 1987 during the anniversary celebrations. By that time the "Canadians" had a number of differences, notably no. 10 had a taller chimney. (D.Trevor Rowe)

119.   Since the line was built, the shingle has gradually been colonised by a variety of very hardy plants, but the landscape is still extremely unusual, with scattered economically-constructed buildings. When viewed from the old lighthouse in 1992, the low profile train was well camouflaged. (M.Turvey)

120.   A new lighthouse became necessary in the 1960s, as the power station grew to eclipse the other. A final view from the old one leaves us with a timeless and scaleless impression of Howey's dream that came true for our pleasure. Regular visits are essential for good dream material. (M.Turvey)

MP Middleton Press

Easebourne Lane, Midhurst, W Sussex. GU29 9AZ **Tel: 01730 813169 Fax: 01730 812601**
If books are not available from your local transport stockist, order direct with cheque,
Visa or Mastercard, post free UK.

BRANCH LINES

Branch Line to Allhallows
Branch Line to Alton
Branch Lines around Ascot
Branch Line to Ashburton
Branch Lines around Bodmin
Branch Line to Bude
Branch Lines around Canterbury
Branch Lines around Chard & Yeovil
Branch Line to Cheddar
Branch Lines around Cromer
Branch Lines to East Grinstead
Branch Lines of East London
Branch Lines to Effingham Junction
Branch Lines around Exmouth
Branch Lines to Falmouth, Helston & St. Ives
Branch Line to Fairford
Branch Lines around Gosport
Branch Line to Hayling
Branch Line to Henley, Windsor & Marlow
Branch Line to Hawkhurst
Branch Lines around Huntingdon
Branch Line to Ilfracombe
Branch Line to Kingswear
Branch Line to Lambourn
Branch Lines to Launceston & Princetown
Branch Line to Looe
Branch Line to Lyme Regis
Branch Lines around Midhurst
Branch Line to Minehead
Branch Line to Moretonhampstead
Branch Lines to Newport
Branch Lines to Newquay
Branch Lines around North Woolwich
Branch Line to Padstow
Branch Lines around Plymouth
Branch Lines to Seaton and Sidmouth
Branch Lines around Sheerness
Branch Line to Shrewsbury
Branch Line to Swanage *updated*
Branch Line to Tenterden
Branch Lines around Tiverton
Branch Lines to Torrington
Branch Line to Upwell
Branch Lines of West London
Branch Lines around Weymouth
Branch Lines around Wimborne
Branch Lines around Wisbech

NARROW GAUGE

Branch Line to Lynton
Branch Lines around Portmadoc 1923-46
Branch Lines around Porthmadog 1954-94
Branch Line to Southwold
Douglas to Port Erin
Douglas to Peel
Kent Narrow Gauge
Northern France Narrow Gauge
Romneyrail
Southern France Narrow Gauge
Sussex Narrow Gauge
Two-Foot Gauge Survivors
Vivarais Narrow Gauge

SOUTH COAST RAILWAYS

Ashford to Dover
Bournemouth to Weymouth
Brighton to Worthing
Eastbourne to Hastings
Hastings to Ashford
Portsmouth to Southampton
Ryde to Ventnor
Southampton to Bournemouth

SOUTHERN MAIN LINES

Basingstoke to Salisbury
Bromley South to Rochester
Crawley to Littlehampton
Dartford to Sittingbourne
East Croydon to Three Bridges
Epsom to Horsham
Exeter to Barnstaple
Exeter to Tavistock
Faversham to Dover
London Bridge to East Croydon
Orpington to Tonbridge
Tonbridge to Hastings
Salisbury to Yeovil
Sittingbourne to Ramsgate
Swanley to Ashford
Tavistock to Plymouth
Three Bridges to Brighton
Victoria to Bromley South
Victoria to East Croydon
Waterloo to Windsor
Waterloo to Woking
Woking to Portsmouth
Woking to Southampton
Yeovil to Exeter

EASTERN MAIN LINES

Barking to Southend
Ely to Kings Lynn
Ely to Norwich
Fenchurch Street to Barking
Ipswich to Saxmundham
Liverpool Street to Ilford
Saxmundham to Yarmouth
Tilbury Loop

WESTERN MAIN LINES

Didcot to Swindon
Ealing to Slough
Exeter to Newton Abbot
Newton Abbot to Plymouth
Newbury to Westbury
Paddington to Ealing
Paddington to Princes Risborough
Plymouth to St. Austell
Princes Risborough to Banbury
Reading to Didcot
Slough to Newbury
St. Austell to Penzance
Taunton to Exeter
Westbury to Taunton

MIDLAND MAIN LINES

St. Pancras to St. Albans

COUNTRY RAILWAY ROUTES

Abergavenny to Merthyr
Andover to Southampton
Bath to Evercreech Junction
Bournemouth to Evercreech Junction
Burnham to Evercreech Junction
Cheltenham to Andover
Croydon to East Grinstead
Didcot to Winchester
East Kent Light Railway
Fareham to Salisbury
Guildford to Redhill
Reading to Basingstoke
Reading to Guildford
Redhill to Ashford
Salisbury to Westbury
Stratford upon Avon to Cheltenham
Strood to Paddock Wood
Taunton to Barnstaple
Wenford Bridge to Fowey
Westbury to Bath
Woking to Alton
Yeovil to Dorchester

GREAT RAILWAY ERAS

Ashford from Steam to Eurostar
Clapham Junction 50 years of change
Festiniog in the Fifties
Festiniog in the Sixties
Festiniog 50 years of enterprise
Isle of Wight Lines 50 years of change
Railways to Victory 1944-46
Return to Blaenau 1970-82
SECR Centenary album
Talyllyn 50 years of change
Yeovil 50 years of change

LONDON SUBURBAN RAILWAYS

Caterham and Tattenham Corner
Charing Cross to Dartford
Clapham Jn. to Beckenham Jn.
Crystal Palace (HL) & Catford Loop
East London Line
Finsbury Park to Alexandra Palace
Holbourn Viaduct to Lewisham
Kingston and Hounslow Loops
Lewisham to Dartford
Lines around Wimbledon
London Bridge to Addiscombe
Mitcham Junction Lines
North London Line
South London Line
West Croydon to Epsom
West London Line
Willesden Junction to Richmond
Wimbledon to Beckenham
Wimbledon to Epsom

STEAMING THROUGH

Steaming through Cornwall
Steaming through the Isle of Wight
Steaming through Kent
Steaming through West Hants
Steaming through West Sussex

TRAMWAY CLASSICS

Aldgate & Stepney Tramways
Barnet & Finchley Tramways
Bath Tramways
Brighton's Tramways
Bristol's Tramways
Burton & Ashby Tramways
Camberwell & W.Norwood Tramways
Clapham & Streatham Tramways
Croydon's Tramways
Dover's Tramways
East Ham & West Ham Tramways
Edgware and Willesden Tramways
Eltham & Woolwich Tramways
Embankment & Waterloo Tramways
Enfield & Wood Green Tramways
Exeter & Taunton Tramways
Greenwich & Dartford Tramways
Hammersmith & Hounslow Tramways
Hampstead & Highgate Tramways
Hastings Tramways
Holborn & Finsbury Tramways
Ilford & Barking Tramways
Kingston & Wimbledon Tramways
Lewisham & Catford Tramways
Liverpool Tramways 1. Eastern Routes
Liverpool Tramways 2. Southern Routes
Liverpool Tramways 3. Northern Routes
Maidstone & Chatham Tramways
Margate to Ramsgate
North Kent Tramways
Norwich Tramways
Reading Tramways
Seaton & Eastbourne Tramways
Shepherds Bush & Uxbridge Tramways
Southend-on-sea Tramways
Southwark & Deptford Tramways
Stamford Hill Tramways
Twickenham & Kingston Tramways
Victoria & Lambeth Tramways
Waltham Cross & Edmonton Tramways
Walthamstow & Leyton Tramways
Wandsworth & Battersea Tramways

TROLLEYBUS CLASSICS

Croydon Trolleybuses
Derby Trolleybuses
Hastings Trolleybuses
Maidstone Trolleybuses
Portsmouth Trolleybuses
Woolwich & Dartford Trolleybuses

WATERWAY ALBUMS

Kent and East Sussex Waterways
London to Portsmouth Waterway
West Sussex Waterways

MILITARY BOOKS

Battle over Portsmouth
Battle over Sussex 1940
Bombers over Sussex 1943-45
Bognor at War
Military Defence of West Sussex
Military Signals from the South Coast
Secret Sussex Resistance
Surrey Home Guard

OTHER RAILWAY BOOKS

Index to all Middleton Press stations
Industrial Railways of the South-East
South Eastern & Chatham Railways
London Chatham & Dover Railway
War on the Line (SR 1939-45)

BIOGRAPHY

Garraway Father & Son